YOUR KNOWLEDGE HAS VALUE

AF152613

- We will publish your bachelor's and master's thesis, essays and papers

- Your own eBook and book - sold worldwide in all relevant shops

- Earn money with each sale

Upload your text at www.GRIN.com and publish for free

Tuan Tran

How Companies Use Currency Options in Risk Management

GRIN Publishing

Bibliographic information published by the German National Library:

The German National Library lists this publication in the National Bibliography; detailed bibliographic data are available on the Internet at http://dnb.dnb.de .

Imprint:

Copyright © 2015 GRIN Verlag GmbH
Print and binding: Books on Demand GmbH, Norderstedt Germany
ISBN: 978-3-656-94818-6

This book at GRIN:

http://www.grin.com/en/e-book/298380/how-companies-use-currency-options-in-risk-management

GRIN - Your knowledge has value

Since its foundation in 1998, GRIN has specialized in publishing academic texts by students, college teachers and other academics as e-book and printed book. The website www.grin.com is an ideal platform for presenting term papers, final papers, scientific essays, dissertations and specialist books.

Visit us on the internet:

http://www.grin.com/

http://www.facebook.com/grincom

http://www.twitter.com/grin_com

University of Westminster
Westminster Business School

Discuss the general use of currency options in risk management companies can use

Module: International Risk Management

Student name: Tuan Tran

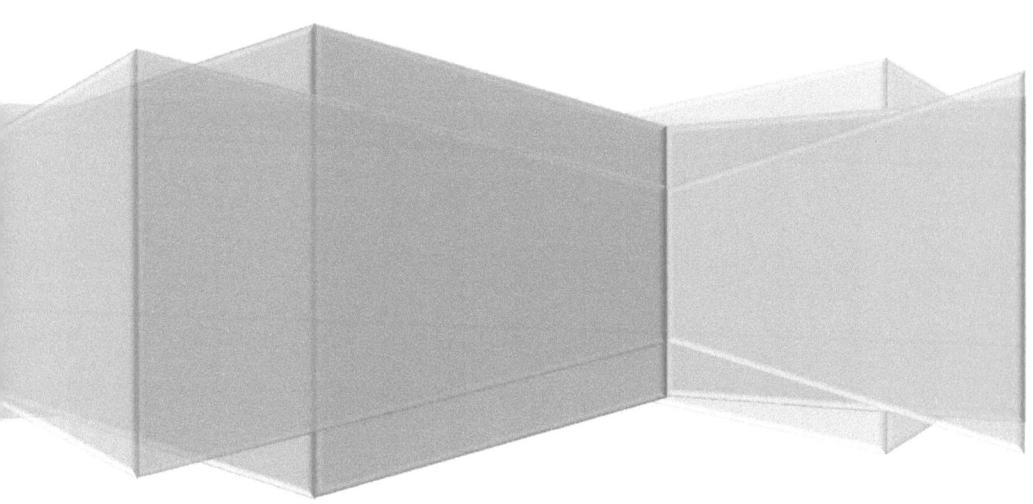

Executive Summary

This article summarizes the motivations behind the reason why many corporates use (currency) options for risk management. Firstly, the paper would generalize the term of Financial Derivatives and how they benefit investors. Furthermore, it review a great deal of previous scholar works done on the field of risk management by corporates and on general options.

In addition, the following case study of the company named ABC using a protective put strategy in order to hedge its investment in BCA is explored in both situation of increase and decrease in share price in order to understand how companies manage risks.

Even though options can be an effective tool that helps companies be successful in grow their firm values options can also become worthless due to a minor modification of share price.

Table of Contents

Introduction

For most of companies, the key of making a sound investment is to maximize profit given a certain level of risk or in other words, to manage risks effectively. Since the 1990s, various studies have proven that risk management was considered by many financial executives as one of the most essential objectives of their corporates (Smithson & Rawls, 1990). Furthermore, with the recent trend of globalization, many new risks arise to a multinational enterprise as it expands their activities aggressively beyond its domestic boundaries. They are now dealing with a variety of issues which potentially involves risks of currency exchange rates, interest rates, overseas political instabilities, material prices etc. As a result, it is reasonable for a multinational corporation to hedge their investments. For example, businesses which conduct series of cross-border activities always have to consider seriously the currency exchange issue since it fluctuates continuously over time and might cause loss to company due to the time lag between the moment contract signed and payment collection. That is the main reason why many corporations with its broad networks globally including IBM or Coca Cola, are engaging extensively in hedging risks by using derivative financial instruments (Allayannis et al., 2001).

Financial derivatives are instruments that have been developed by financial market for decades and now have become popular tools for risk management. In recent time, as the aggressive expansion of multinational enterprises, the utilization of financial tools by these firms is becoming more and more popular with the objectives of hedging against level of exposures. Currently, the market observes four main types of financial derivatives in foreign exchange trading including futures, forwards, swaps, and financial options.

In general, a forward/future contract is an agreement between two parties in which one party, the buyer, agrees to buy from the other party, the seller, an underlying asset or other

3

derivative (in this case, a specific currency), at a future date at a price established at the start of the contract (Chance, 2003). In addition, a company can select another alternative, swap, which is an Over the Counter agreement between two parties to exchange a series of pre-specified future cash flows to gain a comparative advantage (Hull, 2012). Last but not least, buying options equal to buying contracts that give the right, not obligation, to buy or sell an underlying asset (which is a certain currency in this case) (Chance, 2003).

This article would discuss the general use of options as an effective instrument in risk management, particularly in foreign exchange market by revising prior literature and providing a case study as illustration of hedging risk in currency exchange.

Literature Review

1. *Risk Management in Corporates*

According to the theory suggested by Modigliani and Miller, in the world of efficient exchange market, firms should not engage in hedging activities since investors can artificially replicate corporate hedging activities (Modigliani & Miller, 1958). However, hedging against unfavored movements of the market can be justified in the existence of market friction, and in fact, corporates devote a considerable amount of efforts and resources to do so.

To the extent of currency exchange risk, the demand of exchange rate risk management began to arise after the breakdown of the Bretton Woods system which allowed the existence of floating currency rate ((Papaioannou, 2001). Therefore, it is also reasonable for firms to hedge against level of exposures since the volatility of foreign exchange rates can be possibly ten times higher than that of inflation rates and four times higher than that of interest rates (Jorion, 1990). Another rationale explaining why firms actively engage in foreign exchange derivatives is that hedging possibly increases value of firm by decreasing the indirect cost of financial distress, or lessening the underinvestment problem associated with costly external financing which mostly caused by volatility in exchange rate (Froot et al., 1993). By using survey data, the study conducted by (Hagelin, 2003) in Swedish enterprises gave the results which are consistent with the conjecture.

Currency risk management is playing a vital role in every firm's decisions about foreign currency exposure (Allayannis et al., 2001). On the other hand, the study by (Burnside et al., 2001) which examines the possible relationship between macroeconomic condition and companies' hedging policy indicates that it would be ideal for enterprises to hedge their foreign exchange rate completely given no guarantees from government.

2. Hedging strategy and Empirical Literatures

In general, one of the earliest works in this field, (Jorion, 1990) emphasized the possible impact of volatility in currency exchange rate to stock return.

Therefore, recently, scholars dedicated considerable efforts to conduct empirical studies finding the effectiveness of foreign currency derivatives (FCD) in managing foreign exchange risk. Nonetheless, different researches produce contradicted results.

Firstly, (Copeland & Joshi, 1996) and (Hentschel & Kothari, 2001) indicated that there was no existence of such association linked FCD with a lower level of foreign exchange exposure.

In contrast, based on evidence collected from Australian companies, (Nguyen & Faff, 2003) proposed that use of FCD was associated with lower exposures. Furthermore, this hypothesis was supported by study proposed by (Allayannis & Ofek, 2001). In details, by using a sample of non-financial firms in the list of S&P500 for 1993, it found evidence that decision of using FCD for hedging could significantly enhance firm value due to reducing the exchange rate exposures. In other word, enterprises which select FCD receive a substantial hedging premium.

In addition, after studying 720 large non-financial firms in the US in the period of 1990-1995, (Allayannis & Weston, 2001) concluded that firms that used FCD had a higher value of 4.87% than those chose not to be un-hedged.

Further studies suggested that the level of engagement in currency exchange derivatives could vary at different industries since the volatility of exchange rate affected more to industries that were depend heavily on import and export (Bodnar & Gentry, 1993).

(Nguyen & Faff, 2003) confirmed these results by stating in their conclusions that companies in resource sector accomplished a greater reduction in foreign exchange exposures compared to ones in the industrial sector.

3. *Currency Options*

An option contract grants the right, not obligation, to buy or sell an underlying asset (which is a certain currency in this case) during a specified period of time (Chance, 2003). Due to its flexibility, options are one of the most useful instruments that firms use to hedge against adverse movements since the holders are not obliged to buy or sell the asset. Moreover, it is worth noting that 82.5% of market share of all options are took up by currency exchange rate option (Bartram, 2006). The difference between maturity spot price of an option contract and strike price determines whether the trader is better off or worse off.

Many firms use currency exchange options for hedging or speculating purposes, and the following case study would analyse how a call option (to buy GBP) is used to hedge against unfavourable movements.

Case study

1. Background information

Daniel Inc. is a medium-sized company which is supplying raw materials for telecommunication industry and actively operate mostly in the UK market. Recently, it has received some orders from overseas and the buyer prefers to make a payment in US Dollars (USD). The management board of Daniel Inc. considers these orders seriously as this is a great opportunity for them to expand the market. However, this is the first time Daniel Inc. deal with overseas request and they concerns about the recent trend of volatility of foreign exchange market. Assume it is now 12 February 2015 and the company expects a net cash inflow of USD3,000,000 which is due on the 10 May 2015. The executives of Daniel Inc. decide to use financial derivatives to hedge against the un-favoured movement of exchange rate.

2. Alternatives for Daniel Inc.

In this case, Daniel Inc is concerned about depreciation in value of USD or appreciation in value of GBP which can reduce the amount of money in GBP that they are going to receive in the future. In contrast, if GBP depreciates and USD appreciates it would be a favourable change for Daniel Inc. since the value of receipt in GBP will increase. Therefore, Daniel Inc. can select one of the possible derivatives as follow:
- Engaging in a forward/future contract that grants them the obligation to sell USD and buy GBP at a specified price.
- Engaging in a call option for GBP (or put option for USD) that grants them the right (not obligation) to sell USD and buy GBP at a specified price. This type of contract is typically called a USDGBP put since it is a put on the exchange rate or it is equally referred as GBPUSD call.

However, due to the limitation of words, this article will suggest analysis only on the use of one financial tool which is call option. The details will be delivered in the next section.

3. *The strategy*

In this regard, the company is expects to receive a payment worth USD3,000,000 and has the demand to convert the foreign currency (which is USD) to local currency (which is GBP). The current quoted spot rate of exchange is USD1.5119/GBP1.0. In addition, the table below provides the information of option prices.

Strike Price ($/£1)	May Contract (GBPUSD calls) in cent(s)
$1.52/£1	2.48
$1.53/£1	1.95
$1.54	1.49

The executives of Daniel's Inc. declare that they would not make any profit if the value of USD depreciates further than $1.56/£1. Consequently, it is reasonable for them to select the call option with the strike price of $1.53/£1. In addition, to make the calculation to be simpler, we can assume that all options are European-style option which means the holders can only exercise the right at maturity.

Due to selecting the option with the strike price of $1.53/£1, the amount of contracts that Daniel's Inc. needs to purchase is:

$3,000,000/1.53/£31,250 = 62.7 (contracts)

Therefore, the company would take out 62 contracts which is equivalent to $2,964,375. The remaining part of the contract, $35,625 is considered as a relatively minor amount and the risk derived from this amount is probably acceptable for the company.

4. *Scenario 1*

The exchange rate at maturity is $1.5239/£1. As illustrated from the graph, the executive of

Daniel Inc. would be better off to not exercise the call option at this exchange rate. The

details of calculations explaining why it should not exercise its option are listed as follow:

Convert directly at maturity exchange rate ($1.5239/£1)	
Receipt: $3,000,000/($1.5239/£1)	£1,968,633.11
Less: Option Premium 0.0195*$2,964,375/($1.5239/£1)	-£37,932.48
Net Receipt	**£1,930,700.63**
Exercise call options ($1.53/£1)	
Receipt: £31,250*62 contracts	£1,937,500.00
Plus: Convert at spot rate: $35,625/($1.5239/£1)	£23,377.51
Less: Option Premium 0.0195*$2,964,375/($1.5239/£1)	-£37,932.48
Net Receipt	**£1,901,945.03**

On maturity date, if the spot rate stands at $1.5239/£1 which is less than the strike rate of

$1.53/£1 it is obviously out of money and the company should not exercise the call options.

The reason is that it can receive the net amount (after deducting the payment of option

premium) of £1,930,700.53 at spot rate while it would be getting a receipt of £1,901,945.03

after exercising its options. Therefore, the company would be better off to convert its

payment at spot rate.

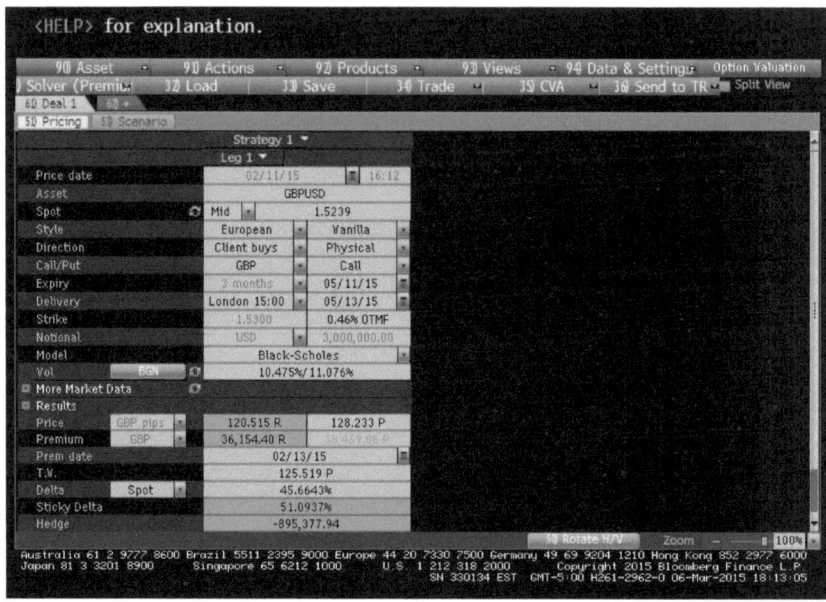

Figure 1: GBPUSD call details. Source: Bloomberg (2015)

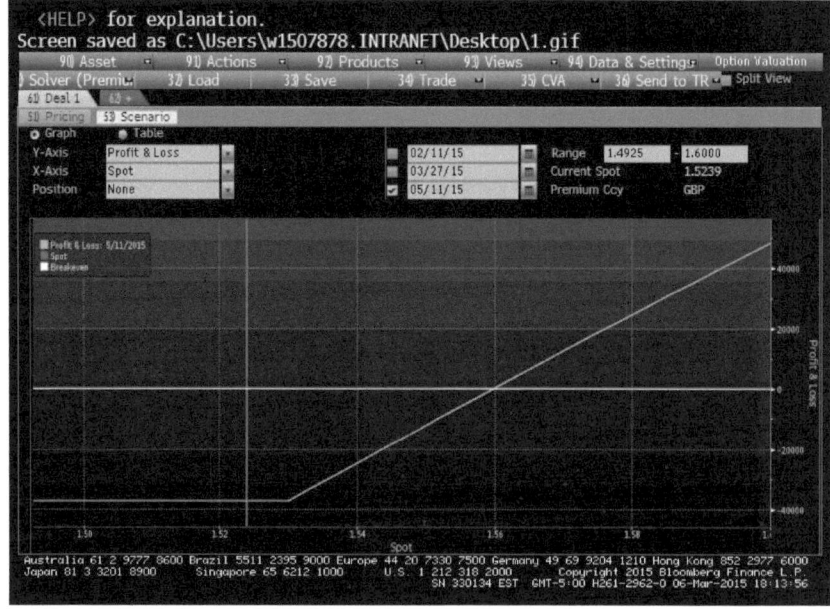

Figure 2: Payoff Graph of Daniel Inc. Source: Bloomberg (2015)

5. Scenario 2

The exchange rate at maturity is $1.5426/£1.

In this situation, the executives of Daniel Inc. would be better off to exercise the call option at this exchange rate. The details of calculations explaining why it should exercise its option are listed as follow:

Convert directly at maturity exchange rate ($1.5426/£1)	
Receipt: $3,000,000/($1.5426/£1)	£1,944,768.57
Less: Option Premium 0.0195*$2,964,375/($1.5426/£1)	-£37,472.35
Net Receipt	**£1,907,295.92**
Exercise call options ($1.53/£1)	
Receipt: £31,250*62 contracts	£1,937,500.00
Plus: Convert at spot rate: $35,625/($1.5426/£1)	£23,094.12
Less: Option Premium 0.0195*$2,964,375/($1.5426/£1)	-£37,472.35
Net Receipt	**£1,923,121.77**

On maturity date, if the spot rate stands at $1.5426/£1 which is higher than the strike rate of $1.53/£1 it is obviously out of money and the company should exercise the call options. The reason is that it is expected to receive the net amount (after deducting the payment of option premium) of only £1,907,295.92 at spot rate while it would be getting a higher receipt of £1,923,121.77 after exercising its options. Therefore, the company would be better off to exercise the options at any maturity spot rate higher than $1.53/£1.

12

6. Benefits and drawbacks of using options

By using options, it grants its holders the flexibility in making decision since theoretically the maximum loss is the option premium (1.95cents per option) and the maximum saving can be unlimited. On the other hand, the drawback of options is its premium cost and its expiration date. For investors, option contracts may expire being worthless and they would suffer a loss of 100% of their investments. In addition, in hedging, firms and investors may end up being incorrect in predicting direction which results a wastes in purchase options.

Conclusions

Although many investors consider currency options market as great speculating opportunities for potential gains it is worth noting that its important role lies in opportunity for firms to hedge against adverse movements. In fact, the volatility of exchange rate after the breakdown of the Bretton Woods possibly results losses for companies which operate or trade internationally since the exchange may direct against the interest of the firm. That is the reason why firms are engage in FCD, particularly currency options in order to minimize the possible loss or hedge the exchange rate risk.

The discussion on the case study of Daniel Inc. illustrated the fact how flexible currency options are. Daniel Inc. would not exercise the option if the exchange rate is not favourable for them and would exercise if the expiry rate goes beyond the strike price.

Although there is evidence suggesting that firms which used currency option hedging resulted having a greater value than those who did not (Allayannis & Ofek, 2001) many scholars proved that the strategy of using currency options did not benefit firms as expected.

In conclusion, the key to any successful hedging strategy is the amount of exposure which is hedged (Kolos, 2005).Consequently, it is crucial that managers should be highly aware of foreign exchange market conditions and adjust risk management strategy respectively.

References

Allayannis, G., Ihrig, & Weston, J.P., 2001. Exchange-rate hedging: Financial versus operational strategies. *American Economic Review*, pp.391-95.

Allayannis, G. & Ofek, E., 2001. Exchange rate exposure, hedging, and the use of foreign currency derivatives. *Journal of international money and finance*, 20(2), pp.273-96.

Allayannis, G. & Weston, J.P., 2001. The use of foreign currency derivatives and firm market value. *Review of financial studies*, 14(1), pp.243-76.

Bartram, S.M., 2006. The use of options in corporate risk management. *Managerial Finance*, 32(2), pp.160-81.

Bodnar, G.M. & Gentry, W.M., 1993. Exchange rate exposure and industry characteristics: evidence from Canada, Japan, and the USA. *Journal of international Money and Finance*, 12(1), pp.29-45.

Bloomber, 20115

Burnside, C., Eichenbaum, M. & Rebelo, S., 2001. Hedging and financial fragility in fixed exchange rate regimes. *European Economic Review*, 45(7), pp.1151-93.

Chance, D.M., 2003. *Analysis of Derivatives for the Cfa Program*. 1st ed. Baltimore: United Book Press.

Copeland, T.E. & Joshi, Y., 1996. Why derivatives don't reduce risk. *THE McKINSEY QUARTERLY*, 1, pp.66-79.

Froot, K.A., Scharfstein, D.S. & Stein, J.C., 1993. Risk management: Coordinating corporate investment and financing policies. *Journal of Finance*, 48(5), pp.1629-59.

Hagelin, N., 2003. Why firms hedge with currency derivatives: an examination of transaction and translation exposure. *Applied Financial Economics* , 13(1), pp.55-69.

Hentschel, L. & Kothari, S.P., 2001. Are corporations reducing or taking risks with derivatives? *Journal of Financial and Quantitative Analysis*, 36(1), pp.93-118.

Hull, J.C., 2012. *Options, Futures and Other Derivatives*. 8th ed. Pearson Education.

Jorion, P., 1990. The exchange-rate exposure of US multinationals. *Journal of business*, pp.331-45.

Kolos, S.P., 2005. *Risk Management in Energy Markets*. Phd Thesis. Austin: The University of Texas at Austin.

Modigliani, F. & Miller, M.H., 1958. The Cost of Capital, Corporate Finance, and the Theory of Investment. *American Economic Review* , 48, pp.261-97.

Nguyen, H. & Faff, R., 2003. Can the use of foreign currency derivatives explain variations in foreign exchange exposure?: evidence from Australian companies. *Journal of Multinational Financial Management*, 13(3), pp.193-215.

Papaioannou, M.G., 2001. Volatility and Misalignments of EMS and Other Currencies During 1974-1998. In J.J. Choi & J.M. Wrase, eds. *International Finance Review*. Emerald Group Publishing Limited. pp.61-79.

Smithson, C.W. & Rawls, W.S., 1990. Strategic Management. *Continental Bank Journal of Applied Corporate Finance*, 1, pp.6-18.